America's Creed

A Red, White & Blue Book

By Dave Racer

Red, White & Blue Books

ALETHOS PRESS LLC
PO Box 600160
St. Paul, MN 55106

A Red, White & Blue Book
America's Creed

ISBN 9780977753417

Bible quotes are from the New King James Version.

http://www.alethospress.com
http://www.daveracer.com

Table of Contents

Welcome to the United Government of You and Me ——— 1

Informed Document Inspired by Faith ——————— 5

What is Culture, or *the* Culture? ——————— 7

So Let's Write a Creed——————————— 9

Truth Exists and It Can Be Observed——————— 19

Genesis 1:1 or Con. 1:1?——————————— 25

Lady Liberty———————————————— 31

Don't I have a Right to be Happy? ——————— 33

America's Creed ————————————— 37

What About the Slaves?————————————— 41

The Right to Self-Govern Is in Jeopardy ——————— 43

About the Author———————————————— 46

Added Feature:
My Response to Pastors Who Say Christian
Political Activism Has No Place in the Church

Page 49

Red, White & Blue Books
The Series

Over time, the publisher plans to release a series of small books such as this one that will highlight historical, political, cultural and theological issues and how they relate. This is the first in the series.

Other subjects around which Red, White & Blue Books are being planned include:

Parental Choice in Education
Big Ideas that Matter
The Judicial Oligarchy
The 21st Century Conservative
Economic Development Folly
Taxing us All
Family
And more....

The reader interested in being notified of upcoming releases should contact Alethos Press LLC:

E-mail: alethospress@comcast.net

Mail:
Alethos Press LLC
PO Box 600160
St. Paul, MN 55106

www.alethospress.com
www.daveracer.com

To contact the author, see page 47.

Welcome to the United Government of You and Me — the UGYM

"Who gave you the right to tell me what to do?" the teenager yelled at the father. "I'm 16 and don't need you telling me how to live my life!"

Wow! How many of us with children have heard such a declaration of independence? How many teenagers have said such a thing? Or, at least, thought of it?

Humans naturally resist authority and yearn for maximum freedom, but time and experience has proven that we all need rules by which to live.

Consider what might happen if each family ran its affairs without rules — any rules. Some try, and the courts and jails have to contend with the messes they create.

As a result of this practical problem — that humans cannot live without rules — we have submitted a part of our lives to governments. So let's step back to the beginning and create one. Let's create the United Government of You and Me — the UGYM.

Where should we begin?

I have an idea. You tell me what you believe about rules and I will write it down. Then I will tell you what I believe about rules and you write it down. Then let's compare lists. If your list is different from mine, well, let's change your list.

"Don't ask me to change my list. I am bigger than you and if you push me too far I will hurt you. No, you have no

1

choice. When all is said and done, in the UGYM, my rules win," I assert.

"But I want to appeal to a higher power," you say.

"What power could be higher than mine?" I ask.

"My superior intellect, that is, my ability to think rationally and logically," you explain.

I have to admit, that thought throws me. As I ponder what you just said, I look in the mirror and see the bulging muscles stretching my T-shirt and notice your skinny, bookish body. "Naw. I'm stronger. I'll make the rules," I say, and begin to hand you my list.

"Wait a minute!" you protest, a little too loudly for me. "I've got another idea."

"Oh?"

"Yes, yes, just a minute," you say, scampering to the bookcase and searching for one particular book. Finding it, you blow the dust away and turn around, holding it up in front of your emaciated little chest. "Let's use this as our guide."

"What is it?" I ask, suspiciously, and quite frankly, because I never bothered to learn to read very well.

"A Bible!" you announce confidently.

I shrink back, my muscles relax and I drop my head. I know what it says because I've been to Sunday school, confirmation and church. I learned the Ten Commandments and about loving God — and loving my neighbors as myself, and I sure love myself.

"Okay, I guess the UGYM could write its rules based on the Bible," I finally and reluctantly answer, knowing that somewhere in that book it says that if weak people like you slap me on the face, I have to turn and let you slap the other cheek, instead of pulverizing you. But I also know that it teaches smart ones like you to treat us duller types with compassion and respect, since we are all the same in the sight of God.

Nations need rules

When nations begin, sometime before their government system gets going, the leaders must decide the rules of government. The philosophy of life that informs those basic rules makes all the difference in the world to the citizens and aliens who live in that nation.

If the rules are written at the whim of the rulers — kings, dictators, despots — and the people are left without appeal, the masses live miserably. Most often they are denied even basic human rights.

As well, if the strongest and wealthiest people draw up the rules and if they have no compassion for the masses, the masses are still left in misery. A vibrant middle class never grows.

If the poor and destitute draw up the rules based on their natural and well-understood tendency toward envy or jealousy, they will destroy wealth creation — or create communism.

A middle ground upon which to base the rules is needed. And a decision must be made about how broad or narrow to make the rules.

Should the rules include a list of everything the government can and cannot do? Should it provide an exhaustive list of the rights and responsibilities of citizens?

How could anyone ever agree on such a thing?

Religious conservatives may try to ban alcohol again. Catholics might demand mandatory meatless Fridays. Scandinavian Lutherans could try to ban fun. Liberals, communists and socialists will move to ban all mention of God and religious belief, except belief in the worship of Mother Earth.

Soon enough we will abandon our drive to write such a governing document and go hire the biggest, meanest bunch of killers we can find to protect us. Or, we can search for a system of beliefs that will unite us as we form our new government system.

3

Red, White & Blue Books

What did America's Founding Fathers do?

Once the colonists had won the Revolutionary War, their leaders saw the immediate need to write a set of rules. This resulted in the Article of Confederation. Quickly seen as too weak, they met again in Philadelphia in 1787 to revise them. Instead, they wrote an entirely new set of rules: The Constitution of the United States of America.

Benjamin Franklin signed that Constitution of 1787. As he left Freedom Hall that day a woman stopped him on the street. She asked him, "What have you given us sir?"

"A Republic," he responded, "if you can keep it."

Informed Document Inspired by Faith

Johnny woke up this morning and before getting out of bed picked up the thin booklet laying on the nightstand. *Let me see*, the young boy thought, *how am I supposed to conduct myself today*? And just like every other morning of his frustrated young life, reading his copy of the U.S. Constitution gave him no answers.

Does the U.S. Constitution tell us how to live?

"Well, it deals with matters of state and of politics," you answer.

"Okay, let's see. What does the U.S. Constitution say about where I am allowed to work today?" I ask.

"Silly, those are matters of commerce and free choice," you sneer.

In fact, no constitution tells us how to live. Rather, through the constitution we tell the government how to "live." And we did not do this based on whim or fancy, but rather, on a well-informed, well-reasoned system of beliefs, beliefs that are rooted in the Holy Bible.

"But doesn't the Constitution forbid a religious test to hold office? And doesn't the First Amendment say something about the government staying out of issues of religious faith?" you ask, getting more confused by the moment.

"Yes, you are right — sort of," I answer.

America does have a creed, you see, and it is quite a religious creed. Most importantly, it provides the philosophical basis for the U.S. Constitution and the state constitutions that followed.

America's creed is summarized in the Declaration of Independence of 1776. On its philosophy the Founding Fathers built our system of government. Its words give meaning to the U.S. Constitution. In fact, without the words of the Declaration, the Constitution is paralyzed and weakened, and left open to the opinion of prejudiced judges.

Religious freedom as expressed in the Constitution, for instance, can only be understood through the prism of the Declaration. Since the Constitution was written to devise a system of government for humans, it is necessary to look to the Declaration to understand how the Founding Fathers saw humans.

A bunch of hicks, weren't they?

"How did the culture of their day affect the writing of the Declaration then?" you ask. "I mean, they were pretty naive people weren't they? Kind of backwards? No TV. No Internet. No flush toilets, for Pete's sake!"

Eighteenth century culture directly affected the Declaration. And the Declaration informed the Constitution. And the Constitution provided guidance to the government. And all of it rested on a specific set of beliefs.

If those beliefs fall into a breach created by a new culture, especially one that is antagonistic to those foundational beliefs, the entire system of American government is put at risk. Such a new system of beliefs at best leaves America with a system of government that only vaguely reflects original intent. At the worst, and the most likely, the ideal of American government will fail.

What is Culture,
or *the* Culture?

Culture includes the beliefs, customs, practices and social behavior of a nation. It encompasses many facets of life — arts (music, literature, art itself); knowledge (enlightenment, sophistication and education); theology, at least the kind that actually influences people; shared attitudes, that is, a set of attitudes that are held somewhat in common.

We speak of the American Culture, Russian Culture, Chinese Culture. We break these down into sub-cultures, many of which transcend political borders — theological distinctions; West or East Coast culture; rural culture; environmentalist culture. And among these we make more refinements and distinctions — culture of the Catholic arts community, an East Coast culture based on preserving the Catskills.

All of these divergent and competing cultures must somehow find a safe home in our complex system of government.

In America, sub-cultures that are antagonistic toward the majority Christian creed owe their ability to continue to try and popularize their antagonistic beliefs to that Christian creed.

In order to maintain its rules and ensure greatest freedom, America stands or falls based on three foundations: its creed, constitution and culture — one affects all and all affect one. At times they work in agreement, and at other times they war against each other. And hostile forces,

Red, White & Blue Books

unfriendly forces, constantly press against them, to destroy them and replace them with a new creed, new culture and a new form of government — and not necessarily a new "nation conceived in liberty and dedicated to the proposition that all men are created equal..." (Abraham Lincoln)

The Gettysburg Address
November 19, 1863

Four score and seven years ago our fathers brought forth on this continent, a new nation, conceived in Liberty, and dedicated to the proposition that all men are created equal.

Now we are engaged in a great civil war, testing whether that nation, or any nation so conceived and so dedicated, can long endure. We are met on a great battle-field of that war. We have come to dedicate a portion of that field, as a final resting place for those who here gave their lives that that nation might live. It is altogether fitting and proper that we should do this.

But, in a larger sense, we can not dedicate — we can not consecrate — we can not hallow — this ground. The brave men, living and dead, who struggled here, have consecrated it, far above our poor power to add or detract. The world will little note, nor long remember what we say here, but it can never forget what they did here. It is for us the living, rather, to be dedicated here to the unfinished work which they who fought here have thus far so nobly advanced. It is rather for us to be here dedicated to the great task remaining before us — that from these honored dead we take increased devotion to that cause for which they gave the last full measure of devotion — that we here highly resolve that these dead shall not have died in vain — that this nation, under God, shall have a new birth of freedom — and that government of the people, by the people, for the people, shall not perish from the earth.

8

So Let's Write a Creed

We cannot begin writing our new constitution until we know what we believe. And what we believe is our creed, and in many ways our creed is affected by the culture, and at the same time affects the culture.

We can find self-evident clues about the common creed of America's Founding Fathers by reading what others wrote to them and what they wrote about themselves.

> The commission to Christopher Columbus, prior to his sail westward, is from "Ferdinand and Isabella, by the grace of God, king and queen of Castile," etc., and recites that "it is hoped that by God's assistance some of the continents and islands in the ocean will be discovered," etc.

Christopher Columbus, was sent in 1492 by the "grace of God" and with "God's assistance."

The first charter of Virginia, granted by King James I. in 1606, after reciting the application of certain parties for a charter, commenced the grant in these words:

> We, greatly commending, and graciously accepting of, their Desires for the Furtherance of so noble a Work, which may, by the Providence of

9

> Almighty God, hereafter tend to the
> Glory of his Divine Majesty, *in propa-*
> *gating of Christian Religion to such*
> *People, as yet live in Darkness and*
> *miserable Ignorance of the true*
> *Knowledge and Worship of God*, and
> may in time bring the Infidels and
> Savages, living in those parts, to human
> Civility, and to a settled and quiet
> Government; DO, by these our Letters-
> Patents, graciously accept of, and agree
> to, their humble and well- intended
> Desires. [Emphasis added]

King James told the Virginia settlers that their primary
mission was to propagate, that is spread and teach, the
Christian religion to those people still living in spiritual
darkness.

One of the earliest documents signed by those who
came to the new world was agreed to aboard ship before the
Pilgrims stepped ashore at Plymouth Rock. It's the 1620
Mayflower Compact. This is what our Founding Fathers
wrote on that tiny ship:

> In the name of God, Amen. We, whose
> names are underwritten, the Loyal
> Subjects of our dread Sovereign Lord,
> King James, by the Grace of God, of
> England, France and Ireland, King,
> defender of the Faith, e&. *Having*
> *undertaken for the Glory of God, and*
> *Advancement of the Christian Faith*,
> and the Honour of our King and
> Country, a voyage to plant the first
> colony in the northern parts of Virginia;
> do by these presents, solemnly and
> mutually in the Presence of God and

> one of another, covenant and combine
> ourselves together into a civil Body
> Politick, for our better Ordering and
> Preservation, and Furtherance of the
> Ends aforesaid..." [Emphasis added]

There is more to the Compact, but these are the key words.

It is true that not all of America's earliest settlers came for the purpose of advancing the Christian faith. Some came because the New World offered them a chance to get rich. Some came to flee persecution, or perhaps, a domineering wife. Yet even these who came with wrong motives were subjected to a culture that was based on Jesus Christ.

Those hearty souls at Plymouth Rock interpreted life in the context of Christian faith — more specifically, Protestant Christian faith. The mention of Protestant faith is not intended to slight any other religious preference. It is, quite simply, historically correct.

> In the charter of privileges granted by
> William Penn to the province of
> Pennsylvania, in 1701, it is recited:
> "Because no People can be truly happy,
> though under the greatest Enjoyment of
> Civil Liberties, if abridged of the
> Freedom of their Consciences, as to
> their Religious Profession and
> Worship; And Almighty God being the
> only Lord of Conscience, Father of
> Lights and Spirits; and the Author as
> well as Object of all divine Knowledge,
> Faith, and Worship, who only doth
> enlighten the Minds, and persuade and
> convince the Understandings of People,
> I do hereby grant and declare," etc.

Penn wrote that happiness required religious faith and worship, and that God authored it.

Prior to the writing of the Declaration, Delaware lawmakers in 1776:

> ...required all officers, besides an oath of allegiance, to make and subscribe the following declaration: "I, A. B., do profess faith in God the Father, and in Jesus Christ His only Son, and in the Holy Ghost, one God, blessed for evermore; and I do acknowledge the Holy Scriptures of the Old and New Testament to be given by divine inspiration."

In Delaware, a distinct religious test — a confession of faith in Christ — was required to hold office.

Just after the Revolutionary War, Massachusetts wrote its constitution. From...

> ...articles 2 and 3 of part 1 of the constitution of Massachusetts, (1780:) "It is the right as well as the duty of all men in society publicly, and at stated seasons, to worship the Supreme Being, the great Creator and Preserver of the universe. * * * As the happiness of a people and the good order and preservation of civil government essentially depend upon piety, religion, and morality, and as these cannot be generally diffused through a community but by the institution of the public worship of God and of public instructions in piety, religion, and morality:

> "Therefore, to promote their happiness, and to secure the good order and preservation of their government, the people of this commonwealth have a right to invest their legislature with power to authorize and require, and the legislature shall, from time to time, authorize and require, the several towns, parishes, precincts, and other bodies politic or religious societies to make suitable provision, at their own expense, for the institution of the public worship of God and for the support and maintenance of public Protestant teachers of piety, religion, and morality, in all cases where such provision shall not be made voluntarily."

Massachusetts saw Christian religious faith as so essential to freedom that in its constitution it demanded that taxes be raised for the support of "institutions of the public worship of God" and to pay teachers of faith.

"Hey, that ain't the way it's supposed to be," you protest.

"Oh? Why do you say that?" I ask.

"Because the Supreme Court said that government could have nothing to do with religion," you proclaim, as though you knew something that I did not.

"Oh, did it? Well, that's not how they saw it in 1892. Here's what that court said in the 1892 decision, Holy Trinity vs. United States," I explain, confident that I am about to blow your mind.

> There is no dissonance in these declarations [about America being Christian in nature]. There is a universal language pervading them all, having one mean-

> ing. *They affirm and reaffirm that this
> is a religious nation.* These are not indi-
> vidual sayings, declarations of private
> persons. They are organic utterances.
> They speak the voice of the entire peo-
> ple. [Emphasis added]

The Protestant tenet that salvation comes only through faith in Jesus Christ, and that pursuing that relationship is not subject to any earthly government, provided the strongest motivation for coming to the New World. The Christian faith, they knew, teaches that standing before God, the person who has been redeemed by Christ stands equal with all others, no matter their race, gender, ethnicity, former religious persuasion or even their former life of debauchery and barbarism. Even those redeemed humans who had been forced into slavery still stand equal before God's throne. Each person stands equal under the judgement of the law and each person stands equal in satisfying the law's requirements only through the blood of Jesus Christ. These are patently Christian teachings.

And the outpouring of their Christian faith, as it was already expressed in the laws of nature and of Nature's God, and the Common Law, found their roots in the Christian concept of the "fruit of the spirit." These attitudes result from the way a Christian lives his or her life and they set a proper context for the making of laws based on maximizing liberty: "love, joy, peace, patience, kindness, goodness, faithfulness, gentleness and self-control." (Gal. 5:22-23)

In fact, the opposite of the "fruit of the spirit," which the Christian calls "the works of the flesh" includes conduct that leads to lawlessness: "adultery, fornication, uncleanness, lewdness, idolatry, sorcery, hatred, contentions, jealousies, outbursts of wrath, selfish ambitions, dissensions, heresies, envy, murders, drunkenness, revelries, and the like." (Gal 5:19-21)

Furthermore, since Christian faith can be taught by the community but only accepted or rejected individually, Christianity also offers the best model for tolerance of non-Christians. In fact, the evangelical zeal of Christians naturally draws them to love non-Christians in the hope of guiding them toward faith in Christ.

These ideas set the stage for citizen government. America's creed at the beginning was largely Protestant Christian. And the Christian persuasion continued to have its influence for decades past the writing of the American constitution.

Does this mean that every person who settled in the New World — every leader, every writer, every merchant, every landowner, even every slave owner — was a Bible-thumping, professing Christian, a person saved by faith and heading to heaven? No! A resounding no!

Being the first Americans no more made them Christians than being in a harbor made them a ship. Still, ships are often found in harbors, just as those first Americans, and for generations to follow, were most often found to be Christians.

Once again, the 1892 Supreme Court tried to settle the debate when it wrote:

> If we pass beyond these matters to a view of American life, as expressed by its laws, its business, its customs, and its society, we find everywhere a clear recognition of the same truth. Among other matters note the following:
>
> The form of oath universally prevailing, concluding with an appeal to the Almighty;
>
> the custom of opening sessions of all deliberative bodies and most conventions with prayer;

the prefatory words of all wills, 'In the name of God, amen;'

the laws respecting the observance of the Sabbath, with the general cessation of all secular business, and the closing of courts, legislatures, and other similar public assemblies on that day;

the churches and church organizations which abound in every city, town, and hamlet;

the multitude of charitable organizations existing every where under Christian auspices;

the gigantic missionary associations, with general support, and aiming to establish Christian missions in every quarter of the globe.

These, and many other matters which might be noticed, add a volume of unofficial declarations to the mass of organic utterances that this is a Christian nation.

Christians and a Christian world view dominated all aspects of culture and government at America's founding and for 150 years thereafter. A Protestant Christian world view gave direction to the new nation.

"I get it. You're claiming that those early Americans had a common faith," you say, face lighting up with the joy of discovery.

"Yes, and it so informed everything they did, that they even included it in their beliefs about government," I

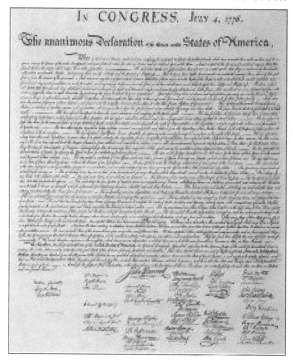

answer, smiling. "And it carried over to the writing of the founding documents."

The key to understanding America's founding lies in the Declaration of Independence, the document that sets forth America's creed; the beliefs upon which it was built. It summarizes the foundational principles, defined before a successful constitution could be written.

Truth Exists and It Can Be Observed

In any gathering anywhere in America at any time, at least where terrorists or thugs have not attacked, there is a sense of order and self-restraint. That is a self-evident truth. Though in any such gathering, at least outside of a church, there are vast differences in theology, we still respect certain principles of freedom and respect. Whether or not we are conscious of it, those principles inform our behavior toward each other. They are embodied in the Declaration.

America's creed states, "We hold these <u>truths</u> to be self-evident... "

America's creed is based on the idea that truth, absolute truth, does exist and furthermore, that it can be observed.

Absolute truth rests on absolute values — a patently religious principle. Faith, science and logic validate the truths. The truths expressed in the Declaration are expressed in the Christian Bible, and it is these truths to which the Founding Fathers ultimately appealed. They are often referred to as Judeo-Christian values, but only because the New Testament flows from the Old Testament. At their basis, these are Christian values — absolute values that are based on a Christian understanding of the Holy Bible.

Since about half of the 56 men who signed the Declaration had been trained in seminaries, it stands to reason that their Christian ideas would greatly influence the document.

Christ often talked about truth — absolute truth. "I am the way, the truth and the life. No man comes to the Father but by Me." (John 14:6) Access to God, Jesus said, has but one entrance and He is it.

In another place He said, "You shall know the truth and the truth shall set you free." (John 8:32) Freedom in this lifetime and in eternity rests on the absolute truth that Jesus Christ paid for our freedom, though He does not speak here of political or civic freedom. The absolute truth is that knowing Jesus gives freedom, no matter the form of earthly governing systems.

"What is truth?" (John 18:38) Pilate asked Jesus, thinking no such thing as absolute truth existed. But it does. Christ is truth.

The same God who inspired the Gospel writers also inspired Paul to write in a letter to Roman Christians about absolute truths — self-evident truths — that can be seen in nature.

> For the wrath of God is revealed from heaven against all ungodliness and unrighteousness of men, who suppress the truth in unrighteousness, because what may be known of God is manifest in them, for God has shown it to them. For since the creation of the world His invisible attributes are clearly seen, being understood by the things that are made, even His eternal power and Godhead, so that they are without excuse. (Romans 1:18-20)

The fact that God exists is a self-evident truth, and so the Founding Fathers believed. And since God is true, then He can be counted on to provide mankind a moral code by which to live. On that moral code can be built a creed. The Founding Fathers built on the creedal foundation of the laws of nature and of Nature's God; not on reason, logic, Freudian psychology, Oprah or the Republican or Democratic Party platforms.

It is self-evident and an absolute truth that God also gave mankind good minds from which logic and science can be applied by godly fear to create wisdom. Solomon wrote about it as his final conclusion in the book of Ecclesiastes. He had studied everything, trying to come to an understanding about life and in the end he wrote, "Let us hear the conclusion of the whole matter: Fear God, and keep his commandments: for this is the whole duty of man." (Ecc. 12:13)

The wisdom that can be drawn from science, logic and reason, if applied in the context of the fear of God, could then be used to better mankind's human condition, if mankind could be freed from government oppression.

Some truths, however, seemed so self-evident to the Founding Fathers that they did not need mindless, endless evaluation and debate. They were beyond argument.

One self-evident truth is that "all men are created — equal." "You have to get through the Creator to get to equality," so says Dr. Alan Keyes, Chairman of The Declaration Foundation.

The act of creation and procreation is a self-evident truth. Scientific, measurable, predictable and without debate, when a woman's egg and a man's sperm unite, human life is the result.

The creation of human life, said the Founding Fathers, is a result of a decision by the "Creator." He set it in motion. Human life, they saw, did not evolve out of some primordial slime. It flowed from the decision of a Creator, not simply by the union of humans in a sex act.

Certainly it is self-evident that the physical union of men and women produce babies, if they are allowed to live to term and be born into the world. That is beyond dispute. Still, the Founding Fathers saw clearly that human life flowed from the hand of God.

The fact of the Creator creating life carried with it certain responsibilities for those He created, among which was the need to respect the Creator's wishes. The Founding Fathers believed that His wishes were expressed on the pages of the Holy Bible. They freely accepted the Holy Bible as an essential guide to daily life, including the design and operation of their governing systems — and in their courts. And why not? They believed in absolute truth and saw there was no better source than the Bible.

Based on their understanding of self-evident (that is, absolute, observable) truth, the Founding Fathers built their creed on inalienable rights. Absolute truths produce inalienable rights. Truth that is subject only to man's reason, manipulation and public polls, produces alienable rights.

Inalienable rights are God-ordained rights.

Inalienable rights are rights that cannot be transferred or taken away, over which humans have no ultimate control They came by virtue of being created, that is, by virtue of being human.

Alienable rights depend on the fancy of a ruling class and they can be easily snuffed out.

"Did you breathe today?" I ask.

"Well, of course. I wouldn't be sitting here reading if I failed to breathe!" you answer.

"Where'd you get that right to breathe?"

"I dunno. It just happened," you answer, not sure where I'm headed.

Breathing is an inalienable right. No human gave us the right to breathe. No human can force us to breathe (except by using a breathing tube forced down our throat). We never asked to breathe. We cannot transfer our right to breathe to someone else. No human can legally take away our right to breathe unless we have surrendered that right by, say, murdering someone else.

The Founding Fathers did not list the inalienable right to breathe in the Declaration, although they implied it. They said that humans are " ... endowed by their Creator with certain inalienable rights; that *among these* are life, liberty and the pursuit of happiness." [Emphasis added]

The Founding Fathers listed only three inalienable rights. They did not say there were only three inalienable rights. Saying so would be denying self-evident truth.

This foundational self-evident truth — that we all have been given the inalienable rights to life, liberty and the pursuit of happiness by God, not by the hand of man — is drawn from the Bible. It is not the invention of a social scientist or pop culturalist trying to manufacture a faith system. Karl Marx could not create it, nor deny it. Neither could Thomas Jefferson. None of us could change this absolute truth if we put our whole life into it, as many tyrants have tried to do.

God gave life. God imbued human life with inalienable rights. He did not do the same for animals, birds, trees or rocks. Inalienable rights belong solely to humans. God gave human life sacred value when He breathed His spirit into man's flesh.

To suggest that God played no role in human life and that, in fact, human life is but an accident of time, means there are no inalienable rights. That, however, is a self-evident lie.

Gen. 1:1 or Con. 1:1?

Here we arrive at a great dividing line.

There are those who have devoted their entire lives to the idea that all life is a result of accidents of nature. Their bible, if they had one, would start this way: "In the beginning, gas." We cite the book of Confusion, Chapter 1, Verse 1 (Con. 1:1).

Those who sincerely believe in Con. 1:1 say that human life is the result of nothing more than exploding gasses becoming matter. Matter then took on life forms. Some of the life forms became fish that walked, while other fish became plants. Some walking fish became apes and somehow, apes became men and women. This evolutionary belief requires a very strong faith system that denies self-evident truth.

Those who place their faith in Con. 1:1, where everything was created by chance, who believe that there is no God, or at least there is no God who created humans, have their own form of religion. And their form of religion is totally incompatible with the American system of government, just as much as is that of the most radical anti-American terrorist.

The evolutionist's faith system rests on the idea of the fittest and strongest of a species surviving at the expense of the weaker members of the species. Its faith claims that the strongest of species will destroy the weaker species. Only the strong survive. In such a world, might makes right and humans are ultimately incapable of taking care of themselves. To them, the only exception to this fact, that the stronger will dominate the weaker, is when Mother Earth flexes her destructive muscles and does everyone in — or an asteroid hits the earth. And it is a system of belief that demands a strong government to make up for the weakness of people.

If the Con. 1:1 environmentalist world view dominates, the end result will always be the same. In time, the strongest will dominate the weakest. Freedom will fail, falling to the hands of the most despicable tyrant who has the largest airplanes to fly into the tallest towers. This is the inevitable result of a system created by chance and run by apes; certainly not by God.

Thank God we didn't start that way!

"I don't like the idea of the big bullies running things," you say, carefully eyeing my 6'5", 265 pound mass of protruding muscle.

"Hey, nature created me this way. And besides," I gloat, "you can trust me — really."

But you don't buy it.

When Thomas Jefferson penned the words "inalienable rights" he had in mind Genesis 1:1 — "In the beginning, God... " God, he and the other Founding Fathers saw, authored human life; actually all life. And in so authoring life, God gave order to His world, a world ruled by humans.

God gave humans dominion over all creation — the land, seas and all forms of life. He set eternal life in the heart of mankind, and a natural urge to find the answer to the question, "Why are we here?" This is simply another way of asking, "How can I know the Creator?"

God also gave mankind the ability to make their own decisions about critical issues. And eventually, He codified the rudiments of His order for human life into the Ten Commandments.

The Founding Fathers saw that God created inalienable rights, and that among these were life, liberty and the pursuit of happiness.

When the signers of the Declaration put their pen of approval to the document that said "life," there remained no debate as to what that term meant. It meant human life. It meant that human life had ultimate value, that it was sacred. It had such high value that Jesus Christ gave His life to pay for the weakness and rebellion of men and women. And as such, humans had a right to live, one that could not be wrenched from them as they walked down the street at the whim of a thug or outlaw. Nor could it be stolen away by an anxious doctor who was being pushed by an even more anxious heir to kill a sick old lady on her deathbed. Nor could the Founding Fathers see that anyone would play God with the human life they carried in the womb by determining that it had no right to live.

America's Founding Fathers understood that humans have nothing to do with their own birth. No human can refuse their own conception, nor can they refuse to enter the world. At the appointed time, it lays beyond the scope of human choice to stay in the womb. Forces beyond the baby's control cause the physical changes that thrust that young child out of the mother into the cold world.

The only exception to this inalienable right to life came from one person's assault on the life of another through murder or, in the case of a capital crime, in the state putting that life to death.

"Whoever sheds man's blood, by man his blood shall be shed; for in the image of God he made man," God told Noah (Gen. 9:6). There are good-willed differences of opinion by people of faith about capital punishment, and this essay is not the place to debate them. Let it stand as fact: At the time of America's founding, capital punishment fit their world view, and their world view was Christian.

God, the author of life, placed supreme value on human life. Therefore, as the Founding Fathers debated their creed, that is, the system of beliefs upon which they built their laws, they saw human life the same way God saw it — as supreme and of such great value that the Son of God gave His life for it.

The belief in the supreme value of individual human life profoundly affects the way governments govern. Those who see humans in light of various classes of people govern the less privileged classes with brutal force. Since they see that all humans are not equal, contrary to God's natural law, they see that classes of humans can be treated unequally; some with privilege and respect, long lives, castles, mansions; and some with dangerous, short lives lived in squalor, hovels and caves.

Some see human life as an expendable commodity, so they send boys into battle to preserve their barbarism, strap bombs to 10-year old girls and call them weapons, or send them flying into tall buildings to assert their claims to a higher principle.

Still others see some human life, that of the unborn child, as non-human and so send in scissors, knives and forceps to kill that life and wrench it from the womb.

When a nation has crossed a line that no longer protects the inalienable right to life, it has opened up whole new possibilities for alienating all rights, or acting as the gods that decide what rights each person retains. These human gods decide what constitutes human life and they add to this the role of deciding the quality of life for those they allow to live. No longer are they the protectors of life; they become the arbiters of life, and as such, also decide who should be granted what kinds of liberty.

If America casts off the Founding Fathers' creed based on self-evident truth and inalienable rights then the discussion of human liberty and the pursuit of happiness is meaningless. Only those humans allowed to live or who exercise their right to decide who will live can have any hope for liberty, and that liberty will always be threatened by those who have more power and might.

"I don't want anyone messing with my inalienable rights," you now say. "I don't trust no human ..."

"Any human... "

"Right, any human to play God with me," you say with conviction. "Goodness, I can hardly trust the politicians to vote right about unimportant things. Why should I trust them with my liberty if they can't be trusted with my life?"

"You're catching on," I smile. "So let's make the inalienable right to life a centerpiece of our new government for the UGYM."

"Right on!" you shout.

Lady Liberty

"Do you think humans were born to be free?" you ask.

"Good question. The Founding Fathers certainly did," I answer. "They said that God gave us the inalienable right to liberty."

Liberty might be defined as the freedom to think or act without being forced to do so — thinking and acting because we want to think and act. As we slipped out of the birth canal into the light of the world, despite the fact that we never asked for it, God gave us the freedom to think or act without being forced to do so. That is the way the Founding Fathers saw it.

Humans are born to be free independent creatures, unoppressed by tyrannical governments. Humans are born to enjoy maximum freedom.

Did the Founding Fathers, then, believe that humans could live without restraint? Certainly not. Practical observation, that is, self-evident truth, shows that human nature requires restraint, because natural man, without God, tends toward selfishness and brutishness. So their observation was that man should be governed by voluntary restraint, not dictatorial restraint; by submission, not submersion; by restraint entered into voluntarily.

Humans have the ability to give up some of their liberty to preserve all of their liberty.

"I think I should have maximum liberty to swing my fist anywhere I want to," I assert.

"Well, your freedom to swing your fist ends at my nose," you say.

The very idea that humans, created as equals, have an inalienable right to individual liberty flew in the face of contemporary governments of the Founding Fathers' day. But the Christian world view of the Founding Fathers demanded this of them.

They knew that Peter had written about freedom to the suffering Christians of his day. "For so is the will of God, that with well doing ye may put to silence the ignorance of foolish men: As free, and not using your liberty for a cloak of maliciousness, but as the servants of God. Honor all men. Love the brotherhood. Fear God. Honor the king." (1 Peter 2:15-16)

Christians understand the concept of absolute liberty and the idea of voluntary submission to authority, and they know that these two not only are compatible but absolutely necessary for mankind to achieve earthly happiness.

In the Founding Fathers' world view, where you came from, your gender, or status in life mattered nothing. "There is neither Jew nor Greek, there is neither slave nor free, there is neither male nor female; for you are all one in Christ Jesus." (Gal. 3:28)

God's Gospel message has been extended to all humans, and so is His inalienable gift of liberty to be extended. We can, and often do, argue about how Christ's gift of salvation is given to all men, but as believers, we do not argue this fact: that in offering His salvation, God draws no lines of distinction. Democrats, Republicans, Greens, Socialists, Communists, Islamists even, can find God's grace reaching out to them through the Gospel of Jesus Christ.

The essential issue of the equality of all humans and their inalienable right to liberty is rooted in the Founding Fathers' Christian world view.

Without human life, liberty means nothing. Without liberty, the pursuit of happiness would fail. Man cannot be happy in this life without having the liberty to pursue his own dream, with minimal governmental resistance.

Don't I have a Right to be Happy?

The Founding Fathers wanted to create a useful creed in as few words as was necessary. They said that the Creator endowed humans with inalienable rights, and that among these were life, liberty and the pursuit of happiness. Happiness means different things to different people, and perhaps that is their point: No government can determine for any individual what will produce human happiness, but government sure can get in the way and prevent happiness by telling people how to live.

When Jefferson wrote the words "pursuit of happiness," the people of his day knew what it meant, and they knew of one of its most important applications. That may not be so true in modern America.

Today, many see the *pursuit* of happiness as, instead, the *guarantee* of happiness. They think that God gave them the right to be happy instead of the inalienable right to *pursue* happiness.

"Wait just a minute there," you say. "You're one of those who are going to say that the government should stay out of giving people handouts, aren't you?"

"Well, yes, I am, but... "

"And you're going to say that some people should be allowed to accumulate a lot of stuff while others have to live on very little, aren't you?"

"Right again," I answer, hoping this doesn't end our attempt at forming a new government.

"But I don't get it. If government's not supposed to

help us with all this, then who is?" you demand to know, tapping your foot and cocking your head, as though you caught me at some failure in logic.

Government cannot create happiness; nor can it create wealth, health, liberty or life. But it can work to protect all these human pursuits.

The Founding Fathers debated the words of this third inalienable right. They knew they could make a long list of inalienable human rights, but chose to condense them into this one term. Their use of this method of description is helpful in understanding how they wrote the Constitution 11 years later.

When they wrote the Constitution, they assumed that people understood that all rights belonged to the people, except for those they voluntarily gave up to the government. These rights, called enumerated rights, were written into the Constitution to tell the government what it should do to protect the inalienable rights of citizens.

One of those rights that sat highest on that list was the inalienable right to own property and earn a livelihood. They saw it as an inalienable right of humans to produce by the sweat of their brow that which would sustain them, build their own estate and then pass their estate on to their heirs. Human happiness in great part came from enjoying the fruit of their labor.

At an even deeper level, they saw the truth of Scripture. "As for every man to whom God has given riches and wealth, and given him power to eat of it, to receive his heritage and rejoice in his labor — this is the gift of God. For he will not dwell unduly on the days of his life, because God keeps him busy with the joy of his heart." (Ecc. 5:19-20)

Man was born to work, to provide for the family, to store up for the future, to provide for old age, to leave something behind for his children. This is an essential aspect of the pursuit of happiness.

Man is born with the inalienable right to work, to pursue property, to own his salary, to own the things his salary, or income from earnings, will bring to him. But man's happiness does not come from what work produces but rather, from the work itself. That is what Ecclesiastes says: Man rejoices in his labor.

"Okay, here I think you are nuts," you say sarcastically. "I hate my job."

"Really? Do you feel good at the end of a work day?" I ask.

"Of course. I get to go home. Work's done," you say, crossing your arms, thinking you've got me now.

"When you think back on the day — at least, most days — how do you feel about the quality of your work, or the quantity of the work you did that day?" I ask.

"Pretty good, usually. I mean I have some bad days, and then ... "

"And then, what?"

"I try to make up for it the next day," you frown. You want me to know you feel happy about a job well done, even if your job involves mostly menial work.

"So you can't deny it. You feel good about doing a good day's work, even if you hate your job," I assert now, with a clever grin on my face.

"I suppose so," you grudgingly admit, "but I really would rather do something else."

That is the beauty of America. If you really want to do something else, and you have the intellect and motivation to do so, you can achieve almost anything. Age, infirmities and issues beyond your control can, of course, frustrate your efforts. But there is a great joy in pursuing one's dreams, even when they are not totally or ultimately realized – the pursuit brings joy.

And when those dreams are realized, we look back on the struggle to succeed with a sense of fondness, even when the struggle felt brutal as we went through it. The Founding Fathers saw the wisdom in the struggle to achieve the ownership of property; they saw that it was an inalienable right.

During the struggle of work, we acquire property for our labor — a salary, or wage — that we will apply to meeting our needs. We experience joy as we care for ourselves and for our children. We find, in fact, that we prefer to live this way, rather than having someone take care of all our material needs. In fact, one of the greatest joys of human life, the joy of giving, is made possible by the accumulation of property.

Once again, the Founding Fathers could turn to a guiding principle from the Bible. This is often referred to as Biblical arithmetic: Too much plus too little equals just enough. "For I mean not that other men be eased, and ye burdened: But by an equality, that now at this time your abundance may be a supply for their want, that their abundance also may be a supply for your want: that there may be equality: As it is written, He that had gathered much had nothing over; and he that had gathered little had no lack." (II Cor. 8:13-15)

Without having the inalienable right to gain property we would be denied the opportunity to meet the needs of others. The result would be physical poverty on the part of the needy one, and spiritual poverty on our part. The Apostle Paul said it again as he was talking to the elders in the church at Ephesus. "I have showed you all things, how that so laboring ye ought to support the weak, and to remember the words of the Lord Jesus, how he said, 'It is more blessed to give than to receive.'" (Acts 20:35)

This creed, of the right to own and enjoy the product of one's own labor, drove Americans to make immense progress, taking us from the agricultural economy, to the industrial economy and on into the information economy. And it caused the Founding Fathers to design a system of government in which charity rested with the people, not with the government.

America's Creed

Humans, guided by the hand of Divine Providence, understood as their predominant world view that there is a Creator and that He created. In so doing He bestowed on humans certain rights. They start with the sanctity and supreme value of individual human life. This is followed by maximum human liberty with millions of individuals making thousands of individual decisions daily about how to pursue their own goals and dreams.

This, then, is America's creed. And it is best expressed in the Declaration of Independence. Without the creed, the Founding Fathers could not have written a successful, enduring Constitution, and it is in the light of this creed that we should view the Constitution.

"So what do you think?" I ask.

"I like this a lot better than having the brutes make all the decisions, that's for sure," you answer, emphatically shaking your head in agreement.

"And I like it a lot better than having just the smartie pants deciding everything," I answer.

So in the United Government of You and Me, just as in the founding of the United States of America, we have a creed. It is based on the self-evident truth that there is a God, and that He gave us inalienable rights, that those rights start with the supreme value of human life, individual liberty and the right to pursue our dreams — and to own property.

Red, White & Blue Books

But is America a Christian
nation? Or is it a nation
just for Christians?

Let's settle one issue right now. Is America a Christian nation? Or put another way, at its founding, was America a Christian nation? It depends.

Words are used to provide shorthand so we can understand things. The shorter we can make our phrases the better, but we must always try to maintain accuracy in our short sentences. This need to communicate directly affects how one answers the question about America being a Christian nation.

Of the 56 signers of the Declaration, half were graduates of seminaries. These were Christian seminaries, not Islamic, or Jewish or those of Reverend Moon. And they were Protestant seminaries that saw life through the prism of a Christian world view. It is a safe assumption that 28 signers at least had a Christian world view. Evidence suggests that of those remaining, all but two had what we today might label a Protestant Christian world view.

Consider the two men usually identified as the least religious of the Founding Fathers.

Ben Franklin is often identified as a Deist. The modernist would think that meant that he believed in a creator, but not one who was directly involved in daily earthly events. Yet it was Franklin who stood up at the Constitutional convention and pled with the other members to stop and pray to God for the new government.

Franklin was but one of six who had been present at both the signing of the Declaration and of the Constitution. He told the delegates at the Constitutional convention that during the time of the writing of the Declaration, there had been daily prayers to the Almighty for protection and guidance. And the Declaration attests to this in its references to

Divine Providence and the Supreme Judge of the Universe.

As Franklin spoke that day, he had been troubled by the disagreements that threatened to dissolve the convention. He quoted from the Book of Psalms. "Unless the LORD builds the house, they labor in vain who build it..." (Psalm 127:1) He reminded the delegates that God numbered the hairs on their heads and knew when each sparrow fell to the earth. He urged them to pray. Why? Because Franklin knew that without God's blessing there would never be a nation of free people.

Does Franklin's admonition, given during the last part of his life, sound like the words of a man who thought God played no role in the affairs of man? Not at all. Did he express here a Christian world view? Yes, right out of the Psalms and the Gospels.

The other founding father often pointed to as a non-Christian, the other Deist, is Thomas Jefferson.

We always think of Jefferson as the author of the Declaration. The Declaration was written by a committee of five men, and debated vigorously. Jefferson wrote the draft and made the amended changes, then wrote the final copy and, of course, served as the country's third president.

There is no question that Jefferson played a significant role in the building of our great republic. And it seems as though Christian faith played a lessor role in his life that of George Washington, John Adams or many of the others. And it is to Jefferson that many point when discussing the so-called constitutional separation of church and state. To many, Jefferson was, at best, a Deist if not an agnostic. And it seems likely that at different times in his life, he believed differently.

Yet, on January 9, 1816, in a letter to Charles Thomson, Jefferson wrote that he had put together a "wee" book, as he called it, which he titled The Philosophy of Jesus. He told Thomson he did this to show, "That I am a real Christian," and added that he was "a disciple of the doctrine of Jesus."

Joshua Cohen, during the mid-1850s, edited a book about Jefferson's Biblical writings. In the introduction he explained why Jefferson had written what he had titled "The Morals of Jesus." According to Cohen, Jefferson decided to present the parables of Jesus in a way that the Indians could understand. Furthermore, Cohen asserted that Jefferson's ultimate goal was to present Christ, the Savior, to the Indians.

It may be true that applying a fundamentalist Biblical definition of "Christian," we would find that Jefferson and Franklin failed. They may even be spending eternity in hell. Let God be their judge, not us. But from Jefferson's own writings we can only conclude that a Christian world view at least played a significant role in his life.

Were we founded as a Christian nation? The learned members of the U.S. Supreme Court in 1892 certainly believed so. Does such a term mean that all men, or that predominantly, the Founding Fathers meant to create a nation where the tenets of Christianity must be accepted? Yes, that, too, seems clear. It is very clear that America's founding and its creed, all that informed its writing of the Constitution, its laws and the operation of its courts; all this was singularly dominated by a Christian world view.

The Founding Fathers' Christian world view states that we are created by a Creator, and that He gave us inalienable rights: life, liberty and the pursuit of happiness.

What About the Slaves?

"Hold on just a minute," you say, suddenly having another thought. "Those Founding Fathers were virulent racists, white Europeans whose sole intent was to rape and pillage the new land, and do it on the backs of Africans stolen from their homelands and forced into slavery."

"You better look closer before saying this," I caution.

When Jefferson wrote the first draft of the Declaration, one of the charges he brought against King George was that the king tolerated the slave trade. He condemned the king for this. Unfortunately, and admittedly a black mark on our founding, politics played a role in removing that statement from the Declaration. In order to get representatives from all 13 colonies to sign, that statement was deleted from the final draft of charges. But, by the fact of its original inclusion, we can see that men of good will challenged slavery even during the tense and explosive political debate at our beginning.

It would take another 85 years for slaves to gain the inalienable right to liberty, and they got it because white Christian men of principle continued to press the fight for their freedom.

John Quincy Adams, our sixth president, upon completion of his presidential term, ran for Congress and won. And for 14 years he pestered the Congress to end slavery.

The Emancipation Proclamation, the Civil War, passage of the 13th Amendment, all of this resulted from one

thing: the Christian notion of the equality of man, whether black, white, red or yellow.

"Jesus loves the little children. All the children of the world. Red and yellow, black and white, they are precious in His sight. Jesus loves the little children of the world," so goes the Gospel song.

America became the champion of ending slavery throughout the world. Our creed, of inalienable rights, needed to be exported to every land and every people. And it is the same creed that drove America's civil rights leaders to keep on fighting for equality.

Someone asked Alan Keyes during his 1996 presidential campaign why it was that at the beginning, Americans treated black slaves as inhuman. His response, paraphrased: "That's simply not true. Read the Constitution. It said that at our founding slaves were to be counted as three-fifths of a person. Three-fifths is not a whole person, but it still meant they saw them as humans; as people."

Reading what the 14th Amendment states as it regards the so-called property of the slaveholders demonstrates that the majority of Americans refused to acknowledge that slaves were property. It did this by denying slave owners the right to collect one single dollar for the loss of their slaves. America had imposed its creed on slave owners. Will we see the day when Americans apply the same rigorous judgement on those who commit abortions, who prosper from the taking of innocent human life? Only if Americans reassert their faith in idea of the supreme value of human life.

The Right to Self-Govern is in Jeopardy

One more aspect of the Declaration creed must be discussed. It forms an essential aspect of the American system of government — that the right to govern comes from the consent of the governed. Citizens, the Founding Fathers believed, have the right to choose their own systems of government. These cannot be chosen by tyrants, dictators, central parties, national denominational leaders, Congress or the Courts; but by the citizens.

Building a government based on this creedal belief of self-government was, at that time, a revolutionary idea.

America's creed, the Declaration of Independence, is a creed built upon a Christian world view. It is a true representation of the underlying foundation upon which all other American institutions are built. Without informing our understanding of the Constitution by the creedal utterances of the Declaration, we will fail to understand, and we will fail to maintain our Constitution. That, in fact, is what has happened.

In July of 1787, another group of Founding Fathers gathered together to sign the Northwest Ordinance of 1787. The ordinance was written to provide guidelines for governing the Northwest Territories out of which six states were eventually carved.

This signing preceded that of the U.S. Constitution by two months. George Washington was one of those who signed the ordinance, and among other things, it banned slavery in the new territory.

From that ordinance: "Paragraph 13: And for extending the fundamental principles of civil and religious liberty, which forms the basis whereon these republics, their laws and Constitutions, are erected...to fix and establish those principles as the basis of all laws, Constitutions, and governments, which forever hereafter shall be formed in the said territory."

The laws of the territory were established to guarantee civil and religious liberty. Why? Because they were the foundation upon which our republic was formed, upon which were written our Constitutions and upon which was written our system of laws! This cannot be any clearer.

Yet, many modernists, even many in our pulpits, confuse us with a hollow debate about whether or not we were or are a Christian nation. We are a nation founded by men and women who had a distinct, clear, conservative, comprehensive, Christian world view, that they lived, breathed and upon which they depended. Upon the foundation of this world view grew the most powerful and free society in the history of the world.

The Founding Fathers, in their brilliance and in their honest dealings with the hearts of men, went even farther in the Northwest Ordinance. They reinforced the idea and established the principle of a nation ruled by educated citizens, but not educated in a moral vacuum. In fact, they strongly implied that a free people had to be saturated with moral teachings:

> *Religion, morality, and knowledge* being necessary to good government and the happiness of mankind, schools and the means of education shall forever be encouraged. [Emphasis added]

These men stated clearly that one of the duties of territorial government was to teach religion, morality and knowledge. They understood that "the fear of the Lord is the beginning of knowledge, but fools despise wisdom and instruction." (Prov. 1:7) Compare this truth as promoted by our Founding Fathers with the commonly accepted modern principle of the separation of religion from governmental affairs.

It is instructive as to the thinking of some modernists that during 1997, a school board in Michigan actually seriously considered removing the reference to religion from the Northwest Ordinance, fearing it violated the so-called constitutional separation of church and state — 210 years after George Washington had signed it into law. These Michiganders feared the Northwest Ordinance violated some absurd notion that religion should be separated from governance.

Should those who believe that the Christian religion has no role to play in government succeed, the end result is that a different religion will predominate. Today it is the religion of Secular Humanism that sees humans as the center of everything, not God. Eventually it will result in the dividing up of our land as we lose a common religious faith, and it will give way to the strong-armed tribal tactics of an American Ayatollah.

"I prefer life, liberty and the pursuit of happiness to oppression," I say.

"Me too," you agree.

"Because, I fear God, and I see you nodding your head in agreement."

About the author

Dave Racer

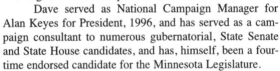

Dave and his wife Rosanne live in St. Paul, Minnesota and have five children and two grandchildren.

Dave has written more than 19 books. He has also edited other published books, written pamphlets, teaching materials and opinion columns.

Dave served as National Campaign Manager for Alan Keyes for President, 1996, and has served as a campaign consultant to numerous gubernatorial, State Senate and State House candidates, and has, himself, been a four-time endorsed candidate for the Minnesota Legislature.

Dave wrote and produced 34 editions of "Dave Racer's Minnesota Report," a monthly tabloid newspaper (1987-1990); has written and produced more than 300 radio commentaries; hosted a daily and weekly talk radio show, *The Dave Racer Show*, from 1990 until 2001 on Twin Cities radio stations. He has designed, and manages, several websites.

Dave teaches American Government and Student Senate at Y.E.A.H. Academy in Roseville, Minnesota.

Dave is the founding President of The Declaration Foundation, Inc. and the Chairman of The Declaration Project. He is also the President of The Constitution Educational Foundation.

The current list of Dave's written work (2006):

*Your Health Matters: What You Need to Know About
    US Health Care*
In the Shadow of Joseph
Caged Bird
Death by Design
Two weeks that will last Forever
The Senator's Son
Cardinal Chronicles: Part I - Prescription for Death
To Change the Heart of Man
American Christians and Government
Real Public Education: The Parents' Choice
Smokie's Last Job
At the Cross Series:
        Sarah of Bethlehem
        Bartimaeus Sighted
*NOT FOR SALE The Rev. Sun Myung Moon &
        One American's Freedom*

Dave served as senior editor for these books:

Leviticus v. Leviathan, by Wayne B. Holstad, J.D.
A Treatise on Human Life, An Unalienable Right,
        by Harold Kletschka, M.D.
Minnesota Injustice, By Dale Nathan
Foundations of Freedom, by Art Mathias
*Choices, Designing an Eternal Landscape,
        The Tom Bever Story*
My Journey with Cancer, by Mabel Olson

To contact Dave Racer, write to:
Alethos Press LLC
PO Box 600160
St. Paul, MN 55106

www.alethospress.com
www.daveracer.com

Red, White & Blue Books

Added Feature:
My Response to Pastors Who Say Christian Political Activism Has No Place in the Church

July 30, 2006: *The New York Times* and *The St. Paul Pioneer Press* published an article about the ministry of Pastor Greg Boyd, founder and senior pastor of an evangelical mega-church in the Twin Cities. Pastor Boyd preached a series of six sermons last summer that he incorporated into a book in which he defends his decision not to preach about political issues, such as abortion, homosexual marriage, and the global war against terrorism.

I received links to the article from a relative of mine who does not agree with my Christian conservative politics; I also received the article from a long-time Republican activist who, on other occasions, had expressed his dislike for Christian activism in political parties. This, then, is my response to these two.

It would be interesting to me what theme you embraced by reading about Greg Boyd's opinions. Did you, for instance, like the idea that he does not equate Christian with Republican? Support for Christ with political support for the president? Or was it that he wants to focus on the Gospel of Jesus Christ? If it was the latter, then I cheer the article and your view of its message.

There are some things to admire about Boyd's message (as far as the article reveals it, having not read his book).

He proclaims that faith in Christ is the ultimate issue, for if hearts are not changed to this life-giving message, then all other intentions count for nothing. In fact, without the message being Christ-based, the agenda can and often does become hard-edged, mean, and unfounded in fact - then it is simply an emotional message.

The church's primary mission is not to teach about ending abortion, protecting traditional marriage, or winning the global war against terror. The mission of the church is to teach the whole Word, present the Gospel, equip believers, and administer the sacraments. Yet the church also must teach Christians to be salt and light. (Jesus said this, and I imagine Pastor Boyd agrees with that assertion.)

The church in which I had my membership for 59 years tends to avoid these same themes, refuses to hand out voters' guides, features no politicians, has removed the U.S. flag from the worship center, and as much as possible, never equates party politics with faith in Christ.

There is one glaring factual error in Pastor Boyd's message, and there is a huge failure in his mission to teach and equip his members and church attendees. The same is true of my former church.

First, the secular doctrine of constitutional separation of the church and state is without factual basis. This assertion is a relatively recent assertion of the U.S. Supreme Court, dating to the Everson v. U.S.A. decision of 1947, and followed by ever-worsening interpretations. The Court, in fact, directly contradicted itself in numerous subsequent decisions, and tried to expunge the "Holy Trinity" decision of 1892. That decision, in fact and with total clarity, asserted the unique Christian nature of our constitutional form of government and our history.

Second, and this is more troublesome for me, Pastor Boyd's assertion about the church and these issues considers U.S. citizenship to be a separate issue from Christian faith. I am of the firm belief that my faith is a 24-hour, 7-day, lifetime commitment, and must form a part of who I am, whether in politics, work, leisure, church, or the grocery store. Christian faith is not reserved for the pews on Sunday.

America's Founding Fathers saw each citizen as sovereign. We were not to turn to kings, or emperors, or dictators to rule us. No, we look to ourselves, expressing our will through elected representatives, to carry out our will at the local, state, and national level. This means that, without question, every U.S. citizen has a role to play in government, and that includes Christians – even, evangelical and Catholic Christians.

Christians have a right and a responsibility to be involved in our unique, constitutional republic. Our right is no greater or lesser than that of atheists, liberal mainline Christians, Jews, Muslims, or any other people of faith. We have a right and responsibility to help mold the policies of our nation, states, cities, and neighborhoods.

When the Bible talks of marriage, the church should teach it. When the Bible talks of sexual purity, the church should teach it. When church members join together at political party caucuses to express their will upon the political process, they should not be enjoined from speaking publicly about what they believe, based on the Word. If, in so doing, they are elected to office, they cannot and ought not to leave that faith in the pews. And if, because they speak plainly, the public refuses to vote for them, so be it.

One final point, and that has to do with the public display of the U.S. flag in a church worship center; some, like Boyd, see this as setting up an idol in the place of God, or as some implicit endorsement of Christian faith as being uniquely American. Others, like me for instance, see public display of the flag in a worship center as an acknowledge-ment of God's blessing on our nation, His sovereignty even over our earthly rulers, and a remembrance of the shed blood of those Americans who gave their lives so that we might live in peace.

For me, then, the issue of Christian faith and the church is the Gospel of Jesus Christ; and the purpose of the Christian life, no matter the context, is to express that faith everywhere by how one lives and communes with others.